D0924267

How to
Make Money
Selling Art
at Auction

How to Make Money Selling Art at Auction

Trade secrets and insider advice from an art market expert

Anthony R. Westbridge

Illustrations by Kirsti

Westbridge Publications Ltd.
2000

Copyright © 2000 by Anthony R. Westbridge

All rights reserved. No part of this publication may be reproduced, stored in a retrieval system, or transmitted in any form or by any means, electronic, mechanical, photocopying, recording or otherwise without prior permission of the publisher.

Canadian Cataloguing in Publication Data

Westbridge, Anthony R.

How to make money selling art at auction

ISBN 0-9685907-5-6

1. Art auctions. 2. Painting--Marketing. I. Title.

N8602. W482 2000   750'.688 C00-910509-3

Published by:

Westbridge Publications Ltd.
1737 Fir Street, Vancouver, B.C. V6J 5J9 Canada
Telephone: (604)736-1014 Fax: (604)734-4944
e-mail: info@westbridge-fineart.com
web site: www.westbridge-fineart.com

Author: Anthony R. Westbridge

Illustrations: Kirsti

Disclaimer:
This publication is designed to provide accurate and authoritative information. It is sold with the understanding that the publishers are not engaged in rendering fine art investment, appraisal or other professional advice. If such advice or other expert assistance is required, the services of a competent professional should be sought. The content of this book represents the experiences and opinions of the author, but the author and publisher are not responsible for the results of any action taken on the basis of information in this work nor for any errors or omissions.

Printed and bound in Canada

For Rowena, Nicholas and Allison

Contents

Part One:
The Auction Process

Part Two:
How to Make Money Selling Art at Auction

Part One

The Auction Process

What you need to know before you take your art to auction

Auc-tion *n.*
A public sale in which the price is increased by bids until the
highest bidder becomes the purchaser.

Introduction

How to sell art at auction? How difficult can it be?
Isn't it just a matter of taking the painting to the local auctioneer and - hey presto! - he'll do the rest?

It can be that easy, and for most people, it probably is
- especially if their motive is simply to dispose of the
painting no matter what. A very high percentage of art
works have little or no economic Value, primarily because they are just not good paintings. In these Cases, the
objects have served their purpose - perhaps decorating a
wall for several years - and their 'profit' has been earned
either in the pleasure they have given or the space they
have filled. For these works the auction process is a

charitable way to extend their life expectancy. As an art dealer, I am brought these types of paintings all the time and my answer is always the same: send them to auction - no reserve!

But not all paintings fall into this category. Many works have considerably more than decorative value, and yet, all too often, they also are dropped at the local auction house for disposal, with little thought for their real worth and market potential. If your painting falls into this category and you don't explore its real market potential, then you could be cheating yourself out of a small fortune.

How often do we hear of paintings that sell for very little in a local auction finding their way into the main markets to sell for thousands - sometimes hundreds of thousands - of dollars? Far too often, and it needn't ever happen. Those enormous profits could, and should, belong to the original owner - you!

While these great finds - or losses, as the case may be - are the exception rather than the rule, they do exist. But, more prevalent are those mid-range art works that are neither worthless wall decor nor priceless Old Masters. These are the works on which the art market is built. They make up close to 80% of all auction activity and include paintings in the low hundreds of dollars to works in the several thousands.

Art dealers and serious collectors thrive off this sector of the market. They use their knowledge and market savvy to find undervalued paintings in small auction houses and minor sales and, after careful attention and research, re-direct them to more lucrative and appropriate markets elsewhere.

This book has been written to help you think and see the way the dealers and connoisseurs do. It treats your painting as if you had discovered it in a small, provincial saleroom and guides you in the steps you need to take to ensure you get the best price possible when you re-direct it to another saleroom. When you finish this book, you will be a sophisticated seller of art at auction, and ready to take on your equally skilled and sophisticated adversary - the art buyer!

Art buyers today are more knowledgeable and selective in their buying habits and expect much more for their investment dollar than ever before. As a result, it has become increasingly more difficult for a consignor to secure a strong price at auction for anything other than the rare and exceptional. However, you can substantially increase your prospects of securing a strong price if you follow certain basic rules of the marketplace. Seldom do all the ingredients for achieving a strong price at auction come together in one painting, but it certainly helps if a number of them are in place.

To help you gauge the saleable potential of your painting at auction, I have compiled a list, not in any specific order, of important criteria that I have discovered elicit the greatest market response. But first, there are some facts you need to know about the auction process.

*"The art market is the trading
activity of paintings."*

Chapter 1.

What is 'the market'?

The art 'market' refers to that area of the fine art industry that deals in secondary market, or re-sale,
paintings. It does not refer to the regular gallery scene
unless the gallery deals in secondary market works. More
often than not, because most auction prices are public
knowledge, it is the auction market that forms the price
structure of the art market. Like the stock market, the art
market has its own indices for various schools, periods,
movements, styles and individual artists. Again, because
of the open nature of the auction process, these indices

are almost exclusively based on auction prices. The art market, therefore, is the trading activity of paintings.

The 'market' is also that almost indefinable buying force present at any time when paintings are offered for sale at auction.

It is also important to recognize that the buying side of the art market is usually comprised of a relatively small group of serious collectors and art dealers. These individuals account for the vast majority of the activity within the market. They may not be the final purchasers in all cases, but they will definitely be instrumental in establishing the final price. How they view paintings that are offered for sale at auction, therefore, is extremely important. Their knowledge, expertise, and market influence carries a great deal of weight. A painting that is ignored by the 'trade' more often than not falls short in some significant area of value or interest.

*"once you make the decision to
sell at auction, your painting
instantly enters a totally new
realm of recognition and value"*

Chapter 2.

Is auction right for you?

Selling a painting through an auction can be a very exciting and profitable experience. It can also be stressful and deeply disappointing. While no one can predict the fate of a work offered at auction, much can be done prior to its being put 'on the block' to ensure that the stress and disappointment are kept to a minimum and that the excitement and profitability prevail.

Therefore, the first question to ask yourself is: 'Do I really want, and have, to sell this painting?' That is to say, do you want or need the cash that it will generate, no matter how much that is, more than you want the painting itself. If the answer is yes, then the process is straightforward. You place the painting at auction, without reserve, and sell it to the highest bidder, come what may. Liquidation in this manner is usually reserved for very minor works in local salerooms. If there is an urgent need for the funds the painting will generate, then you might be wise to try and sell it directly to the art trade, or privately, before you go to auction, because salerooms will often take up to a month to pay-out after a sale.

However, if you are only interested in selling the painting if you can be guaranteed a specific amount of cash in return, then a very different scenario comes into play. Your motive for selling is more speculative or profit oriented than it is one of necessity. Now you need to market rather than liquidate. At this point, several criteria come into play - not only to help you achieve the best price possible, but also to ensure that your work is protected against a poor market.

But whether you are simply fishing to see what the market will bear or have an urgent need to sell, once you make the decision to sell at auction, your painting instantly enters a totally new realm of recognition and value. It takes on a whole new identity. From the moment it is consigned to auction until the gavel falls at the end of bidding, the painting belongs not to you - but to the market.

No longer is it for your eyes only, gracing your walls and, hopefully, giving you immense pleasure. Now it is the object of thousands of eyes and intense scrutiny. The financial expectations you might have held for it in your hopes and dreams will have to give way to the vagaries of the market. It will be touched, stroked, poked, bumped, sneered at by some, admired by others, perhaps

10

subjected to the tell-tale rays of an ultra-violet lamp - in short, dissected to the max, all in the interests of finding a new home.

What happens to your painting once it leaves your walls may not be of interest to you. But it should be, because, if for any reason it does not sell and is returned to you, you may think you are getting the same painting back - but you aren't! A painting that fails to sell at auction, according to auction 'lore', almost instantly loses its market appeal, particularly with dealers and serious collectors. It appears to become tainted, almost unclean if you like - and certainly harder to sell at a future date, particularly if it was illustrated in an auction catalogue. The stigma of being "bought-in" at auction stays with a painting for years. Because of its market exposure, art dealers are unlikely to want it after it has failed at auction unless it is offered at a greatly reduced price, and the auction market itself will generally not entertain it again for several years unless it is also at a much reduced price.

Even fine paintings, if mismanaged at their first auction exposure, can end up on the eternal reject heap. Why this happens remains somewhat of a mystery especially when it concerns good pictures. But that is the way it is, and more often than not, such paintings will have to venture to a totally new marketplace if they are to have any chance at all of selling for a reasonable price.

You can see, therefore, the importance of understanding your own motivation for selling at auction. A missed calculation can mean not only a missed opportunity, but also a serious loss of investment value. The purpose of this book is to help you avoid this dilemma.

*"The 'hammer' price may well
be attractive...but what will
the net result of the transaction
be for the consignor?"*

Chapter 3.

The 'hidden' costs of
selling at auction

In recent years, the idea of selling through auction has
become more and more popular. Extensive marketing
by the auction houses since the 1970s and the subsequent
media exposure they have received, particularly following celebrity auctions, have had a pronounced effect on
the overall structure of the art market today. High-end
auction houses are no longer viewed as the wholesale
buying outlets they once were but rather as sophisticated

retail operations that have chosen the auction process as a means of selling their goods.

The price differential, therefore, between goods sold at these auctions and similar goods offered in retail galleries is now almost indistinguishable. Indeed Christie's, one of the world's leading auction houses, claims through its advertising to be "the retail market of choice for buyers and sellers alike."

However, there are still several very significant and important differences between true retail selling and selling through auction. Each has its pros and cons, and each is vital to the ongoing strength and success of the local, national and international art markets. But, because of their current high profile, auctions are attracting more and more consignors anxious to achieve what they believe will be significantly higher prices for their works of art. And these consignors may be right.

Certainly it can often look that way when the gavel falls to close the bidding on their items. The 'hammer' price - the price the item is knocked down or hammered down by the auctioneer when he bangs his gavel on the podium to denote the end of bidding - may well be attractive, but what will the net result of the transaction be for the consignor? There are several "hidden" costs and conditions in the auction process that may be overlooked by the consignor caught up in the excitement, glamour and potential of high returns that the auction process offers.

The following chapters examine some of these costs and conditions so there are no surprises in store for you when you consign your painting to auction.

*"Estimates are a very general,
and sometimes very broad, gauge
of perceived market value. "*

Chapter 4.

Estimates and reserves

One of the main advantages that an auction house has over retail art dealers and galleries is the way it evaluates works for resale. Auction houses work with estimates. Estimates are a very general, and sometimes very broad, gauge of perceived market value. They offer a price range within which the auction house believes, based on knowledge and experience, the object should find a buyer. A painting may be estimated at $500 - $700 or $5000 - $10,000, for instance, or, in the case of major works, perhaps $3 million - $5 million. These are estimates and not guarantees. Dealers, on the other hand, do not have this flexibility. They have to accurately assess and value the work to the very dollar at which they intend to offer it, especially if they are buying the piece rather than taking it on consignment.

The problem with the saleroom estimates, at least from the art dealer's viewpoint, is that they are wonderful lures to get the items to auction, because just about every consignor will always look to the high end of the estimate as the real value of a work. History tells us, however, that most paintings sell either at the low end of the estimate or below. Few ever succeed to their highest expectation. It is very important, when you decide to consign to auction, that you understand this fact.

It is also important to understand that most auction houses will set a reserve on your work if it exceeds a certain value. That value varies with individual salerooms. As a rule of thumb, most auction houses will not consider a reserve on a painting valued at less than $500, and many today are setting the limit at $1000. The reserve is usually somewhere in the region of 80% of the low estimate. For example, if you consign a work to auction with an estimate of $1000 - $2000, then the reserve - the lowest price at which the auctioneer is allowed to sell the piece - will be $800. Therefore, the auctioneer can sell the painting for as little as $800! A far cry from $2000!

So, make sure when you consign your painting to auction that you can live with the reserve price, and treat anything higher that your work might attain as a welcome bonus.

*"you might find yourself paying
the auctioneer for the privilege
of not selling your painting"*

Chapter 5.

Commissions and fees

Using the same example as in the previous chapter - an auction estimate of $1000-$2000 - it is possible and, statistics tell us, more than likely that your painting will sell somewhere very close to its reserve. It is on this selling price, or "hammer" price as it is known in the trade, that the auction house is entitled to take its commission. Do not pay attention to the auctioneer's final published price for your painting. It will almost certainly include a 10% or 15% buyer's premium that is added to the hammer price. This premium is part of the auctioneer's fee or commission for selling your painting, and he collects it directly from the purchaser. You are paid on the hammer price only.

Consignment commission rates vary from auction house to auction house, but as a general rule, you can expect to pay - or have deducted from the sale of your work - the following rates of commission:

On a selling price:

Up to $500	- 20%
$500 to $1000	- 15%
Over $1000	- 10%

Based on this scale, your $800 painting would cost you $120 to sell, netting you $680. In some smaller salerooms, commissions can run as high as 25% and 30% for the lower priced goods. In the major rooms, such as Sotheby's and Christie's, recent published rates have shown a charge of 15% for items selling up to $2000, 10% on items between $2000 and $7500, and 6% for goods that sell between $7500 and $140,000. The sliding scale continues until it reaches 2% for goods selling for more than $7 million. As commission rates can change, and are often negotiable, you should view these figures as a guide only and endeavor to secure the best rate possible for yourself when you consign your painting to auction.

In addition, many auction houses, particularly the larger ones, charge a buy-in fee - usually 5% of the bought-in, or last offered, price - if the painting fails to sell. In our example, if your painting failed to reach its $800 reserve and the last interest the auctioneer had was at $600, you would be charged a buy-in fee of $30.

There might also be a minimum lot charge, usually $50 or $75, which auction houses implement to cover the administrative costs on items not deemed valuable enough to warrant protecting with a reserve price. If your painting falls into this category, make sure you know the auction house's policy before you consign. Otherwise, if your painting fails to sell or sells below the minimum lot charge, then you might find yourself paying the auctioneer for the privilege of not selling your painting or the difference between its selling price and the minimum lot charge.

Either way, it's not a good deal!

*"You will need insurance coverage
while your goods are in transit...
and in the hands of the saleroom."*

Chapter 6.

Shipping, insurance
and other costs

U nless you consign to an auction house in your city,
you are going to incur crating, shipping and, most
likely, insurance costs to get your painting to the
saleroom of your choice. The costs, of course, will de-
pend on which crating and shipping method you choose.
It will be relatively inexpensive if you use cardboard and
styrofoam packaging and a ground shipping service
within your own country. And it will be quite expensive

if you use wooden crates and overnight air express to a foreign country.

In addition, if you are shipping overseas, there are several export, customs and tax implications that you should examine prior to packaging. You will need insurance coverage while your goods are in transit, whether you are shipping within country or internationally. When your work arrives at the auction house, it is usually assessed an insurance charge of 1%-1.5% of its sold value to protect your work while it is in the hands of the saleroom. Some auction houses give you the option of declining this insurance. It would not be a wise decision on your part to do so.

Although, at all times, auction houses take the utmost care of every item on their premises, accidents can happen. The sheer volume of works handled on a daily basis by most salerooms is staggering. Factor into this the number of employees handling goods and number of times an object has to be moved during its saleroom sojourn, and the argument for in-house insurance is clear.

Other costs include photographic charges, if you want your work illustrated in the auction catalogue, and, if the work fails to sell, return packaging and shipping charges from the auction house. Do not expect the auction house to keep your shipping crate for possible return shipment. Therefore, if your painting does not sell, you might incur similar - or even greater - crating and shipping costs to those you paid to send the work.

Make sure you are prepared for this possibility, or you may end up in a similar situation to that experienced by a colleague. He sent a large and extremely heavy 'Old Master' painting to a New York saleroom from the West Coast. The painting failed to sell and it cost more to get the painting back than the work cost to purchase in the first place.

Even dealers can overlook all the hidden costs!

Several auction houses also charge a 5% storage or warehousing fee for works both sold and unsold but not collected within a certain period of time, usually five days to a week following the sale. It is the consignor's responsibility to arrange for the return of his works should they fail to sell at auction.

*"major salerooms require paintings
to be submitted as early as
three months prior to the sale."*

Chapter 7.

Consignment deadlines
and pay-out schedules

Selling a painting at auction, as you can see, is definitely not as simple as it sounds. It can also take a lot
longer than you might imagine. So, if your motivation
for selling your painting is to realize some immediate
cash flow, then the auction route may not be the way to
go for you. Having said this, you will probably find that
most small local auctions will take consignments as late
as a few days prior to the sale. Larger salerooms, and
particularly the major ones, require paintings to be sub-

mitted as early as three months prior to the sale. This allows them to properly authenticate and examine the works, illustrate them if necessary for pre-sale publicity, and research, photograph and describe them in preparation for inclusion in the auction catalogue.

When the sale is over, you might also have to wait quite a while to receive your payment. Again, local and rural salerooms will often pay out as early as ten days after the auction (some, perhaps, even sooner). The bigger rooms, however, will usually take as much as 35 days before they issue you a cheque, which means it might be closer to 40 days after the sale before you can put it in the bank.

So if quick cash is your need, the larger salerooms are definitely not the right vehicle for you.

*"It is difficult for anyone to
accurately assess value and authenticity
from a photograph."*

Chapter 8.

How to approach an
auction house

How do you go about getting a painting to auction?
The easiest way, of course, is to sell it on the local
market. Here, a phone call to the auction house to make
an appointment is the first step. The person in charge of
fine art will then ask you some questions about your
piece - so make sure you have all the necessary information at hand: size, subject, medium, artist, date if known -
and, based on this information, will make a decision.

If your painting is considered to be important enough, the auction house will send a representative to see it. They might also do the same if it is a very large piece and can't be transported easily. However, for the most part, you will be asked to bring the piece in for examination. Occasionally, when the saleroom knows it has no market for a certain painting, you will be told that the saleroom is not interested. Do not be discouraged if your work is rejected in this manner. If other auction houses exist in your area, try them all. One might be less particular or have better luck with your kind of work.

If you are looking to sell your painting outside your local market, then you should take several good photos of the piece and send it, together with as thorough a description as you can, to the auction house or houses of your choice. Always address your correspondence to at least the 'art department'. However, larger international salerooms such as Sotheby's and Christie's, which offer specialty art sales, have several specific divisions within one general art department. You can, therefore, expedite matters more quickly and efficiently if you address your correspondence to the right division for your work.

For example, you may need the Victorian pictures department, or American Paintings, or 18th Century European Pictures, or even Marine or Sporting Pictures. If you are not sure into which specific area your painting falls, then send it to the art department in general, and the auction house will forward it to the appropriate division.

When giving information on the piece, make sure you include not only the size, subject, medium, artist and date, but also the condition. Are there any tears or noticeable damage of which the auction house should be aware? Also, are there any additional marks or labels on the back of the painting that might be of assistance to the auction house in valuing and verifying authenticity of your piece?

Allow at least a couple of weeks to get a reply, especially from overseas. If you are in a hurry, make sure you include a fax number or e-mail address to which the saleroom can respond quickly. It is unlikely that you will receive a phone call from the auction house, especially if it's overseas, unless your painting is very valuable or particularly desirable and the saleroom is anxious to get it.

Once your painting has been accepted, at least in principle based on the photos you have sent, it is then your responsibility to get the painting to them. Locally, there is no problem. However, if you have to ship outside your local region or overseas, the meter starts running and the costs start mounting. First, you should get your painting professionally packaged. You don't have to use a strong wooden crate as in the old days, although that is perhaps still the safest if most costly, method. Cardboard boxes with the proper styrofoam padding are popular materials today. They are strong, light and quick to prepare. You can do the packing yourself, but it is not advisable. Packaging companies have all the right materials and the expertise, and you don't want to risk damage to your painting for the few dollars it would cost for them to do it for you. Furthermore, many insurance companies will not insure goods in transit unless they are packed by a professional packaging company.

Once the piece is ready to ship you can either ask the packaging company to take care of it for you or do it yourself. Air express is usually the quickest and safest way, with the least amount of handling involved. Do not forget to take out insurance to cover any damage in transit. Several shipping companies will not insure paintings, so you will need to do some research to find those that do. If you have a separate fine art floater on your home insurance policy, you might find it covers shipping. Check with your insurance agent. Once you have shipped the painting, it is usually a good practice to send confirmation to the auction house as to when it is expected to arrive and by which carrier.

Upon its arrival, the auction house will catalogue the painting and send you a receipt outlining the details of your agreement with them, such as the pre-sale estimate, reserve, insurance and illustration costs, etc. At this point, when the auction house actually gets to look at your painting physically for the first time, there might be some changes to the terms and conditions tentatively agreed upon with you, either over the phone or in writing. It is difficult for anyone to accurately assess value and authenticity from a photograph. The colors may be different, the condition, when examined professionally, may not be as good as first thought, or, worst of all scenarios, the painting may not be 'right,' or authentic. Once the work has been examined, if changes are to be made to the agreement, you will be notified. If those changes, for whatever reason, are unacceptable to you, you have the right to withdraw the painting from the auction and ask for it to be returned to you - at your cost.

Once examination and paper work are complete, you just have to sit back and wait for the sale to take place. Most salerooms will send you a catalogue both as a courtesy and to prove that your work is included. If you are not able to attend the sale, or choose not to, do not expect the auction house to phone you after the sale to let you know whether your painting sold or not. Life around a saleroom after a sale is sheer pandemonium, and the last thing on anyone's mind is to call consignors with results. On the rare occasion that a saleroom does make a phone call to a consignor, it usually is because his painting fetched a very substantial or unexpected amount, and the auction house wants to be the first to inform and congratulate him. This is definitely the kind of phone call you want to receive!

To find out how your painting fared, therefore, you can either place a phone call yourself the day after the sale or just wait for the mail and see what it brings. Don't forget, the bigger salesrooms take at least a month to pay out after a sale.

So, remember, when you approach a saleroom:

1. Have all the pertinent information about your painting at your fingertips: artist, subject, size of image (not outside frame size), medium (oil, watercolor, pastel, print), date, condition and any distinguishing characteristics, especially old labels on the back of the painting or stretcher.

2. Be prepared to take your painting to your local saleroom if they ask to see it.

3. If you are approaching an out of town or international auction house, send a photograph with all the pertinent information. If there is a lot of information on the back of the painting, it is a good idea to photograph the back as well as the front. You might also want to take a separate shot of the signature to help the auction house determine authenticity and therefore value.

4. If you are going to ship your painting out of town, make sure it is well packed. It makes sense to use a professional packing company, especially if you intend to insure the package. Some shipping companies will not insure goods that aren't professionally packaged.

5. Take out insurance on your package. How much should you insure your painting for? A good rule of thumb would be the low estimate price that the auction house has given you. However, if, in the event of damage, you feel you can justify a higher price, then you would be wise to insure it for the maximum possible. For instance, if you have had a recent appraisal of the piece and it is higher than the auction estimate, insure it for the appraised value.

6. If shipping internationally, make sure you have all the pertinent shipping and customs papers. Check with your nearest customs broker for this information.

7. Send confirmation of shipment, projected arrival time, and name of the shipping company to the receiving saleroom as soon as your package is sent.

8. Be prepared, once your painting has been received by the auction house, for some changes to the agreement you made based on the photograph and information you supplied. When the experts at the auction house have had a chance to examine your painting, they may want to change the estimate, up or down, and, accordingly, also change your reserve if you want one. They may also be the bearers of bad news and inform you that your painting is 'not right.' It happens, so be prepared!

9. Be aware of all the "hidden" costs in sending a painting to auction. You may be asked to pay a 1%-1.5% insurance fee while the painting is in the hands of the auction house. The 1% will be based on the selling price of the painting or its bought-in price if it doesn't sell. You will also have the option to pay for an illustration. And, if the item does not sell, you might be asked to pay

a buy-in fee and a stocking or warehousing fee if the work is not picked up within a short period of time following the sale.

10. Make sure you understand the saleroom's commission charges, and from what figure commission will be deducted - ie. the hammer price.

11. Check the catalogue when it is sent to you or attend the preview if you consigned to a local saleroom. Make sure there are no errors or omissions. If there are, then the auctioneer can make an announcement at the time of the sale or a notice can be affixed next to the painting during the preview. Auction houses also often publish addendums to correct any cataloguing errors.

12. Be prepared to make arrangements to have the work returned to you if it does not sell. You should expect the same kind of cost, or even more, than you paid to send it in the first place. And don't forget the insurance!

*"if you want to insure your painting
against loss, then you will need
a bona fide written appraisal"*

Chapter 9.

Appraisals

Before you ever consider selling your painting at auction, you may be curious to know its current market value and whether it has market potential. There are many things you can do yourself to ascertain this value (see *Part Two, Chapter 11*), but you might want to consider getting the work professionally appraised. You will find independent fine art appraisers in your local phone directory, or you can contact an art dealer or auction house to conduct an appraisal for you. Generally speaking, an appraiser will advise you without charge if your painting is of insufficient value to warrant a written appraisal. Some art dealers and most auction houses will also give you a free verbal appraisal if you take the work to them. This may be all you need to settle your curiosity. However, if you want to insure your painting against loss, then you will need a bona fide written appraisal to present to your insurance company.

When you hire an appraiser, you can request various types of valuation for your art work. The most common is an appraised value for insurance replacement. This is the highest value your work will receive and is generally based on what it would cost to purchase a similar work on the retail market. You can also ask for fair liquidation value, which is what you would receive if you had to sell the work immediately. Appraisers generally look to auction prices for this valuation.

It might seem an unnecessary expense of time and money if you are already convinced you want to sell your painting through auction. After all, the auction house will give you a fair liquidation value pretty much on the spot. But an appraisal does have its advantages, even when you are determined to sell at auction. First and foremost, it will give you a guide as to what you might expect from the auction house. It will also give you a second, and in many cases unbiased, opinion, which can be useful when negotiating with the saleroom. Furthermore, an appraisal gives you a definite insurance value if you have to ship the work. It is also good to have an appraisal in case your painting does not sell and you have to put it back in your collection.

An appraisal is a valuable and important financial document and, as such, should be kept in a safe place along with your other personal and financial documents.

"Markets can be manipulated
by one or two powerful dealers
or collectors"

Chapter 10.

When is the best time
to sell?

A s with any commodity, there is definitely a right and
wrong time to sell art at auction. The same rules apply in the art market as in other financial sectors. Sell
while the market is rising, and buy when it's falling.
Clearly, if you are in urgent need of cash, then any time
is the right time to sell, and you do not have the luxury of
picking and choosing your selling moment. However, if
you are not in a hurry and are anxious to get the best
price possible, then you should pay close attention to

market movements and trends so that you can gauge, as near as possible, the optimum selling time.

One of the best market indicators can be found in newspaper headlines. Historically, when high prices for paintings start hitting the daily press, it seems to follow that we are heading for an uncomfortable dip in the market - perhaps even a recession. It happened in the early 1970s, the early 1980s, the early 1990s - and prices once again are on the rise!

More telling than the daily media are the trade journals. Here you find specific auction results and articles on market trends and prices. Boom periods in any investment market do not last forever, and in the art industry, the gains are generally not as long lasting as in stocks and shares. Markets can be manipulated by one or two powerful dealers or collectors and, in these cases, are only as strong as the controlling influence allows. As soon as the main players withdraw from a specific segment of the market - it may be a single artist, an art group or movement, or even an art period - that segment quickly begins to lose its momentum, demand quickly drops off and prices start slipping back.

Another area to watch is international economic buoyancy. If you are thinking of selling an international work, especially a European or South American work, look to the painting's country of origin to see how buoyant that country's economy is. Buoyant economies create active buying markets for collectors in those countries, and while the economy is hot, auctions around the world featuring those paintings will do well. But when the economy sours - watch out!

Yet another market indicator can be found in the financial success of specific professional groups, such as stock brokers, realtors and, more recently, computer technologists. Historically, when these groups experience rapid growth and success, they invest some of their earnings in the art market. Because these players are more often than not inexperienced and usually enter the market for a single 'play,' they tend to invest in mid range to mediocre works, causing this sector of the market to become overvalued. In many cases, these nouveau-riche investors will recognize their inexperience or perhaps be just too busy making money to have time to participate in the sales themselves, so they will employ dealers on commission to do their buying for them. This creates even more market activity as dealers compete with each other, often for the better quality goods.

When this 'new' money enters the market, no matter the conduit, it means these are excellent times to be selling art!

So, pay attention to the headlines, subscribe to trade journals, and monitor international economies, then pick your moment. The market will do the rest!

*"there may be circumstances where
the purchaser is able to sue the
seller for false information"*

Chapter 11.

Some legal implications
when selling at auction

It is understood that when you sell a painting at auction you have free and clear title to that painting. If you do not and you do not disclose this to the auction house, you could be liable for some serious and expensive repercussions. When a painting is sold at auction the sale transaction

> *"implies that the legal title to the work will
> pass to the purchaser. If it turns out that this
> is not the case - that the consignor is not the*

legal owner of the work, or that a third party
holds a mortgage or other security in the
work - then the sales contract is broken. The
purchaser may then require the auction
house to refund payment."
Art, the Art Community, and the Law
Stephen B. Smart, Self-Counsel Press, 1994, p 99

Over and above clear title to the work, other issues can cause problems for the consignor. Should the consigned painting ultimately turn out to be either a fake or at least not what it was purported to be, then the purchaser can, and usually does, ask the auction house to refund payment.

If sufficient proof is provided to the saleroom - perhaps an expert's opinion or other irrefutable evidence - most auction houses will refund the purchaser's payment without argument. Where the saleroom is not convinced, a legal battle could ensue. In either case, settlement is usually the responsibility of the auction house. However, they could call upon the consignor for reimbursement.

If the dispute over authenticity or provenance is brought about due to false information being supplied by the consignor, then the auction house is well within its rights to come back to the consignor for restitution.

While most transactions resulting from disgruntled purchasers are directed at and handled through the auction house, which acts as agent for the consignor, there may be circumstances where the purchaser is able to sue the seller for false information that affected the value and price of a painting.

The easy answer, of course, is to make sure you own the painting outright or have written authority from its rightful owner to sell it through auction. And make sure the provenance you give the auction house is true to the best of your knowledge. If you don't, it will almost certainly come back to haunt you.

The relationship between auctioneer and consignor

The auction house works for the consignor in the capacity of sales agent for the specific goods consigned. It is, therefore, in the best interests of both parties that the auctioneer try to achieve as high a price as possible for the consigned goods. To this end, as a consignor you may witness what appears to be active bidding on your item as the price climbs close to its reserve. The bidding may or may not be real. Many times, an auctioneer will work the crowd by suggesting that there are actual bids taking place in an effort to initiate some genuine interest among potential buyers. However, unless someone actually steps in and bids or if there are genuine bidders but they do not reach the reserve, the auctioneer will quickly terminate bidding, usually just below the reserve, and move on to the next lot. To the untrained eye, it looks like the work has been sold. It is important to know your reserve so that you can tell whether or not a sale really occurred.

If bidding did not reach the reserve and you did not have an agreement with the auctioneer to sell below the reserve at his discretion, then in the event that the hammer falls at a price below your reserve and there is a legitimate bidder, the auction house has to make up the difference between the bid and the reserve. Why would a saleroom sell below your reserve and end up spending money? More often than not, it is because they will still earn commission from the buyer's premium (which could be either 10% or 15%, depending on the saleroom), and that commission might be worth more than the difference they have to pay to you for selling below the reserve.

Let's take the example of a painting that is estimated at $1000-$2000 and carries an $800 reserve (80% of the low estimate). The auctioneer manages to get the bidding to $750 and decides to sell it below reserve. Based on your contract with the saleroom you will probably have to pay a seller's commission of 15% on your reserve price of $800, which is $120. You would then receive a cheque from the auction house for $680 even though the painting was knocked down for $750. The saleroom takes a 15% buyer's commission from the purchaser, which on $750 would be $112.50, plus they still make $70 over what they have to pay you ($750 - $680 = $70), for a total revenue of $182.50 on the sale of your painting. If they had not sold your painting because it didn't reach the reserve, then no one would have made any money at all!

Check your contract

Make sure you get a receipt for any goods you leave with an auction house for examination or consideration for an upcoming sale. When the auction house agrees to accept the goods for sale, you will receive a contract outlining the terms between you, the seller or consignor, and the auction house, acting as agent on your behalf. Make sure you read and understand the contract thoroughly. If you have any questions about the wording or any of the terms and conditions, get them clarified before the sale takes place. If you wait till after your item has been sold, then it will be too late.

Part Two

How to Make Money Selling Art at Auction

14 money-making
tips to help you achieve
the best price possible for
your painting at auction

"To dealers and collectors, there is a certain magic about a painting that is being offered on the open market for the first time."

———————

Chapter 1.

The painting has to be *fresh* to the market

There is nothing a serious collector or art dealer likes more than to discover a painting that is fresh to the market. By fresh to the market we mean a painting that has never before been seen or offered on the secondary market. It has not appeared at auction or in a dealer's showroom since it was first sold or purchased directly from the artist.

Why is this so important? To dealers and collectors, there is a certain magic about a painting that is being offered on the open market for the first time. Its provenance, or history, is short but known. There is less likelihood, with just one owner, that it has been touched or tampered with in any way. Its image is 'new,' unseen, and fresh, and therefore more desirable. It's almost virginal in its mystery and appeal. All of which means a big premium when it comes under the auctioneer's hammer!

There is a strange unwritten law within the art market - no one seems to know where it comes from - that says a painting has one chance to make a good impression at auction. If it takes that chance and sells according to estimate or better, then it is viewed as a success and its image filed away in the deep archival recesses of every collector and dealer who viewed the auction. It cannot, by that same law, reappear at auction for at least five years, and preferably ten, without suffering the aspersions of the market. "I've seen that one before," or "Oh, that one, is it back again?"

If the painting is not successful at its first auction exposure and is put on the auction block again within a relatively short period of time, then a whole new set of market rules apply. Unless there has been an appreciable shift in market prosperity or, because of its subject, style or artist, it is currently in vogue and therefore desirable and sought after, the painting loses some of its former interest and appeal at its second showing. It's no longer fresh. It's been seen before, perhaps - heaven forbid - even illustrated in a previous auction catalogue!

Everyone - that is to say, from a market standpoint, everyone that matters: i.e. the trade and serious collectors - will remember it if it was illustrated. And, most serious of all, it's now the second time that someone has cast it off. Why? The first appearance at auction is never questioned. The second and all subsequent appearances are.

"What's wrong with it?" Surely the four most damning words a work of art can be subjected to short of being labeled a fake.

First time auction 'failures,' should they appear on the market again within anything less than a respectable time period - say five to ten years - are often subjected to derogatory remarks, ignored by the trade, and almost always carry a lower estimate than before. In the eyes of the market, they are tainted, and their only hope of salvation is to find either an 'unsuspecting buyer' or a bargain hunting dealer or collector at a lower price.

Of course, there are always exceptions to every rule. Paintings will appear at auction even within the same season - and sometimes at the same saleroom, but not usually - and sell for more than before or find a buyer where they couldn't before. This could be due to several factors: poor economy, bad weather, regional interest, better exposure, more prestigious saleroom, and so on. But this is not generally the case. Usually paintings that re-appear too early on the market have to settle for much less in the way of estimates, reserves and buyer interest, than they did their first time around.

Almost fresh is still okay!

While the optimum freshness for a painting is to have never appeared on the market before, almost fresh is still okay! By almost fresh, we mean at least five years between appearances, with ten being more desirable - and definitely not less than three. This allows for changes within the marketplace to take effect: new trends, increased artist popularity, and the arrival of new collectors and dealers. It also allows for other market factors such as overall market improvement, shortage of works, and booming economies.

Being fresh to the market, therefore, is extremely important - just like fresh vegetables on a vendor's stall are always more desirable. To capitalize on the special power and importance such freshness holds, you should make every effort to ensure that the painting sells first time round. Attention to the helpful tips in the following chapters, therefore, is of paramount importance.

Points to Remember:

1. *Previously unseen, untouched paintings are the most desirable.*

2. *A ten year or longer break between auction appearances is most desirable for a painting, five is acceptable, and three is borderline.*

3. *Paintings that don't sell the first time they're offered at auction often attract a negative stigma and will usually carry a much lower estimate the next time they go to auction.*

4. *There are always exceptions to this rule, such as when economies and market trends change, or sometimes when works are redirected to larger, more prestigious salerooms.*

"most bidders, even seasoned professionals, take a pre-sale auction estimate very seriously. A high estimate with a low reserve will often back-fire."

Chapter 2.

Reasonable reserve -
reasonable estimate

As recently as the early 1970s, the major auction houses were still considered, first and foremost, wholesale liquidation outlets and not the more sophisticated, semi-retail centers they have become today. Items were consigned to auction with one purpose in mind - to be sold. Plain and simple. At whatever the market would bear. Reserves and high estimates were practically unknown.

Most auctions were conducted during the day, usually in the morning, and the audience was invariably made up of dealers and serious collectors. Auctions, big and small, were an important source of inventory for the fine art and antiques trades.

Then, in the mid-1970s, Sotheby's changed the whole concept of the auction process. Rather than cater almost exclusively to the trade, it decided to court the same market as the trade - the general collecting public. From a place of commerce, the saleroom turned into a place of entertainment.

Evening and weekend auctions began to appear. Elaborate, high-society previews became the talk of the town, world auction records became newspaper headlines, and the general public got its first taste of the fun, excitement and opportunity that surrounds the auction industry.

Slowly, the fine art salerooms, under the guise of the auction process, were establishing more of a retail than wholesale presence.

Today, the auction has all but eliminated the once proud and prolific secondary market art dealers. To survive, the art trade has had to undergo several dramatic changes. Many dealers have amalgamated to create a more powerful purchasing vehicle. Others have been bought by corporations and now operate as fine art divisions of those multi-nationals. Still others, among them some of the most prominent and long established names in the industry, have simply closed their doors.

For those art dealers that remain today the auction rooms offer an opportunity to earn consulting and acquisition commissions as agents for important clients. Few still use the auctions as serious sources for their desired stock-in-trade.

Power of pricing in the auctioneer's hands

Before Sotheby's turned the auction world upside down with their dramatic move in the mid-1970s, the price of an item put on the auction block was determined by the market on the day it was offered. Today, a sophisticated system of estimates and reserves has put the power of pricing squarely in the hands of the auction houses themselves. They, and not the market, control today's prices.

As a result, the post-1970s auctions experienced their first real taste of buy-ins (BIs) or unsold lots. Goods began to appear at auction with unreasonable expectations. Some caught unsuspecting buyers off-guard, but many were being left unsold.

As we have seen in the previous chapter, one of the most important things to try and avoid when selling at auction is the buy-in. That is having your work left unsold. And without doubt, the most crucial ingredient in whether a work sells or not is its perceived value as advertised by the auction estimates.

Auction estimates - the price range within which the auction house believes the work should sell - are usually arrived at by the saleroom in consultation with the consignor. Because the prime objective of the auction house is to acquire goods to sell, the auctioneer will, more often than not, try and accommodate the hopes and expectations of the consignor in setting the estimate - even when they know the expectations are probably unrealistic.

After all, what do they have lose? With little or no financial interest in the goods they sell, there is no risk to the saleroom in offering over-valued works, except, perhaps, to their reputation when the goods fail to sell. But there is a great risk to you, the consignor!

Don't be greedy.
Buyers take estimates seriously

It is important, therefore, to have and accept realistic expectations. Never lose sight of the fact that most bidders, even seasoned professionals, take a pre-sale auction estimate very seriously. A high estimate with a low reserve will often back-fire. Most buyers will assume that a high estimate carries a high reserve and, therefore, will not even bother to bid. If you are prepared to put a low reserve on your painting, make sure the estimate is in keeping with it.

Don't try and play games with the market - you won't win!

It is important, therefore, to do your homework before you consign your painting to auction. Find out as much as you can about the current market value for your piece. Go to the local library and check the price guides and any old auction catalogues that might be available. Then listen to the auctioneer. While he will listen to what you want, you should also listen to what he thinks. Auctioneers have experience. They know the market. Be guided by their knowledge and suggestions. And if their advice is not what you were hoping for, then perhaps the auction process is not right for you.

While the auctioneer is the one who ultimately sets the pre-sale estimate, you are the one who determines what reserve you want to place on your painting.

The general rule of thumb for placing a reserve - that price below which you have instructed the auctioneer not to sell your piece - is to set it at about 80% of the low estimate. A $1000-2000 estimate, therefore, will usually carry an $800 reserve. Remember: the lower the estimate, and therefore reserve, the more potential buyers you will attract; the more buyers, the more competition; the more competition, the more likelihood you have of your painting not only reaching its expectations but perhaps even exceeding them.

Check with the auction house
on the day of the sale

A very important point to remember is to check with the saleroom either during the auction preview or on the day of the sale itself. Speak to the auctioneer or expert in charge, and find out whether there has been any interest in your painting. At this point, the auctioneer will have one of two answers for you. He will either indicate his confidence in his estimate, which usually signifies that he thinks the painting will sell, or if there has been little or no interest shown in your piece, he may ask you to consider dropping your reserve to give it a better chance of selling.

If this is the case, then you have yet another decision to make. How seriously do you want to sell the painting, and just how important or sentimental is the piece to you? How you answer these questions will determine your response to the auctioneer.

No matter what your emotional attachment to the painting was before you consigned it or what your financial expectations were for it, feelings and needs seem to change once an item is no longer in your possession. Reality often sets in, and you discover that selling the piece is more important than owning it. If this is the case, then you will likely be open to the idea of lowering your reserve. If you are firm on your expectations, the auctioneer will leave the reserve and estimate as they are.

One last point. Never lose sight of the fact that auctions are still perceived as wholesale outlets, even when most buyers know they will probably have to pay retail prices. The very nature of the auction process dictates that you pay as little as is necessary to secure your item. Buyers are always thinking 'bargain.' Therefore, when they come across works that they believe are appraised too highly, they will invariably hold back in their bidding - and you will end up with a BI on your hands.

Points to Remember:

1. *Major auction houses are now more retail than wholesale for both buyers and sellers.*

2. *Unreasonably high estimates can deter even the most seasoned of auction professionals.*

3. *Never try and play games with the art market - you won't win!*

4. *Do your homework. Research the market value of your painting before you consign it to an auction.*

5. *Reserves are usually set at 80% of the low auction estimate.*

6. *Check with the saleroom on the day of the sale to see it your painting has had any special interest or none at all. Ask if the auctioneer thinks you should lower the reserve, and consider carefully all the implications if he does ask you to.*

7. *Drop all emotional attachment to your painting when you decide to sell it at auction, that way you'll be able to think more clearly about its reasonable disposition.*

"Buyers, especially serious collectors and dealers, like to acquire works in as close to their original condition as possible - which means untouched, no matter what."

———

Chapter 3.

Untouched condition

Never! Never! Never!... restore, clean or reframe your painting if you intend selling it at auction. It's a natural reaction whenever one prepares to sell anything, from a used bike to a house, to spruce it up to make it more appealing to potential buyers. In the world of art auctions, 'sprucing up' is a no-no.

Art buyers, especially serious collectors and dealers, like to acquire works in as close to their original condition as possible - which means untouched, *no matter what*!

Why would anyone be more interested in something that is dirty, torn, chipped and showing its age than in something clean, in good repair and more 'presentable'? Lots of reasons!

First and foremost, especially in the case of a potentially important painting, buyers do not want to inherit someone else's handiwork. That handiwork, usually mistakenly referred to as restoration, is more often than not badly performed - which immediately decreases the market value of the work. More important is the fact that serious collectors and dealers have their own experienced restorers who they always use. This way, they know exactly what has been done to the painting to bring it back, as closely as possible, to its original condition.

A keen eye can also spot quality even under dirt and damage. This sparks an interest. Dealers and collectors cannot resist the temptation to see what a painting would really look like once it has been properly cleaned and restored. There is a sense of excitement and expectation in the process that adds value to the work prior to its sale. If all the pleasure of discovery and anticipation has been removed, some of the market's interest in acquiring the work will also disappear.

Works in 'original' or close to original condition also offer a challenge of a different sort, especially if there is no visible signature. Careful cleaning and restoration could uncover a signature or a recognizable style that will allow a firm attribution to be added to the piece. This will enhance its value considerably.

All too often, when someone 'tampers' with a painting before it goes to auction, vital pieces of the painting's history and provenance are disturbed, damaged or lost. This information is usually on the back of the canvas or stretcher bar, or frame. It could be an old exhibition label, the title of the work, a second signature, perhaps a former owner. By repairing tears, cleaning away dirt, and putting on new frames, so much of this vital information becomes lost to us for ever. Retaining this information will almost certainly add interest and value to a work.

Conversely, its absence could have the completely opposite effect and be extremely damaging. Something as simple as the title of a painting could enhance its value several times. It might give us a clue as to the location of a landscape, or the name of the sitter in a portrait, both of which are important to buyers.

Resist temptation of adding a new frame

Ironically, the one cosmetic improvement that most people cannot resist is putting a new frame on a painting. With little thought for their importance or value, old, often damaged or even dull, frames are discarded for something brighter and newer. Wrong! Frames can be restored. And period frames that are original to the work add a whole new value and dimension to the piece.

To many collectors, the original frame is almost as important as a signature. It is part of the painting's history, and damaged or not, it can tell much about a painting over and above any labels or marks that may be on the back. The style of the frame, its coloration, its construction, all play a part in creating a story around the painting that adds value and interest to the work.

Retaining the original frame, therefore, is important. However, if the damage is severe or you just don't like the frame, it's okay to re-frame the painting while it is hanging in your house. But don't discard the old one. Put

59

it away in a safe place just in case the day arrives when you want to sell the painting.

There is another very good reason why you shouldn't touch your painting before sending it to auction. It costs you up-front money! In addition to what you might lose on the auction block because the work has been touched, you have to pay the cost of any cleaning, framing and restoring that you have done prior to going to auction. And that is not cheap! Indeed, you could eventually spend more on preparing the work for auction than you actually receive once it's sold!

So, leave it alone - tears, paint loss, dirt and all! If it's a good painting, then it will find its real market value despite its seemingly undesirable appearance. If it's not a good work, then don't waste your money trying to make it one!

Points to Remember:

1. *Never, never, never restore, clean or reframe your painting if you intend to sell it at auction.*

2. *Any form of restoration can severely reduce the value of your painting.*

3. *Seasoned buyers like to find dirt and grime on pictures.*

4. *Don't remove labels or marks from the back of the painting or its frame. They offer vital clues to the painting's age, authenticity and provenance.*

5. *Always try and save the original frame no matter its condition. Frames can tell an experienced eye some great stories.*

"people buy paintings because of the subject. They like what they see ...it is the image that sells the painting."

Chapter 4.

Interesting subject matter

In real estate, they talk about location, location, location as being the all important ingredient in valuing a property. In the art market, that ingredient might be subject, subject, subject!

It really doesn't matter if your painting is fresh to the market, in untouched condition, and well priced if it has a boring or unappealing subject matter. With very few exceptions, people buy paintings because of the subject. They like what they see. It is colorful or appealing or sentimental or thought provoking. Perhaps it has children or pets in it or is a familiar location. Whatever the reason, it is the image that sells the painting.

Of course, there are always exceptions to the rule. Some collectors prefer to buy 'names,' irrespective of the painting's subject, quality or appeal. For these people, it is the 'who' rather than the what that is important about a work. This kind of collecting shows little taste and is usually reserved for insecure collectors who need to brag about their possessions. However, each to his own. It just means there's a market for almost everything!

Works of a more academic nature also might appear dull or unattractive to the average eye. But to the historian or specialist collector, such works may constitute a major find or be representative of a specific period in a prominent artist's career and therefore have historical or academic value. Again, however, such collectors and situations are the exception rather than the rule.

The rule is - *the subject counts!* And, sometimes, the subject accounts for a great deal. A pleasing landscape can soar in value if the location can be identified. The market immediately expands to incorporate regional collectors, as well as specialists who, perhaps, only buy certain periods and locations of an artist's work. The same is true of portraits. If the sitter is known, it will often enhance the value of the work, especially if the person is important or famous. Generally speaking, collectors like to know the who, what and where of a painting. It makes for more interest, enjoyment, conversation - and ultimately, value.

If you can see a golf course in the painting that's money in the bank!

The subject of a painting can also benefit significantly from market trends. Something as seemingly insignificant as a golf course, for example, in the background of a landscape can send the value of a painting into the stratosphere. Golfing subjects are, and have been for sometime, extremely popular. Haymaking subjects are another 'hot' item, especially in the United Kingdom. Even minor artists can achieve high prices if the subject is right. Other examples include paintings with pretty girls, young children or pets. These subjects have always been highly desirable and will automatically carry a premium.

A premium will also be added to a painting by an established artist if the subject is 'right.' Many artists, especially the better known ones, are recognized for certain specific subjects. It is these that will be of most interest to the market. If an artist is known for his or her snowy mountain landscapes, for example, then a portrait by the same artist, no matter how good it might be, will not have as much market interest or appeal. Consequently, its value will not be as high.

The subject or image, therefore, is extremely important and will play a significant role in the eventual outcome of your work at auction. So, don't worry that your artist is not known or only considered a minor painter. If the subject is strong and the quality present - there is, of course, little value in an appealing subject that is poorly executed - the market will respond.

What if the subject isn't exactly desirable or invigorating? Well, then the stature and reputation of the artist is important. It then may become your only hope!

Points to Remember:

1. *Paintings are purchased, first and foremost, for their subject matter.*

2. *Exceptions to the rule usually involve works by important artists and 'academic' or historically significant works.*

3. *You increase your chances of getting a better price if you can identify the location in a landscape painting or the sitter in a portrait.*

4. *Some subjects are always more desirable than others - pretty women, children, pets - while others might be in vogue at a particular time and therefore command higher prices - golf subjects, haymaking.*

How Do You Make Money Selling Art At Auction?

Don't forget...

1. Quality paintings that are fresh to the market are the most sought after by collectors.

2. Paintings that make a second appearance at auction too soon after their first offering usually have to settle for much less than their original expectations.

3. Unreasonably high estimates will deter even the most seasoned of buyers.

4. Check with the saleroom on the day of the sale to see if you need to adjust your reserve.

5. Never, never, never restore, clean or reframe your painting if you intend selling it at auction.

6. Do not remove labels or any other identifying marks from the back of the painting, stretcher or frame.

7. Paintings are, for the most part, bought for their subject matter before anything else.

8. Paintings that feature young women, children or pets almost always do well at auction.

"The market trades names, not subjects, periods or styles, much the same as the stock market trades companies rather than the products or services they offer."

Chapter 5.

Recognized artists usually ensure a better price

What's in a name? In the art market, a heck of a lot! The greater the reputation of the artist, the greater the chances of selling a painting at auction. A 'name' can still give a glimmer of hope to even the most uninspiring of pictures and will certainly add greatly to the price if the painting is fresh and exciting. It is the name, after all, around which the whole idea of an art 'market' is formed. The market trades names, not subjects, periods or styles, much the same as the stock market trades companies rather than the products or services they offer. Of course, the products or services or, in the artist's case, the paintings, help create the name in the first place.

Because the market trades names, the name is the most important consideration in determining value. An auction house will research the name, relate it to other known factors about the painting, such as size, subject, period and condition, and place a pre-sale estimate on the work which then becomes the perceived value of the piece. Collectors, for their part, can use the name for their own research to make sure that the auction estimate is in keeping with general market interest and values.

Collections are judged by name, not subject

When collectors are asked which works they have in their collections, they always answer with the artists' names. "I have a Constable, a Wyeth and a Renoir." You will never hear "I have a landscape, coastal scene and a Parisian portrait." It is through the names, therefore, that a collection is judged. Ironically, however, it is not generally the name that most collectors are seeking when they go to buy a painting. They are usually just looking for something that appeals to them - "I'll know it when I see it" - or they want a specific subject - perhaps a landscape or seascape - or style. Nevertheless, the interest in these pieces does tend to increase, as does the perceived value, once identity of the artist is known - especially if the artist is famous.

One has to wonder how many of us would have bought Vincent van Gogh's *Sunflowers* if we had seen it in a second hand store and didn't know who the artist was? The same might be said for works of the abstract and pop artists of the 1960s and 1970s. Would we really have purchased these works if the artists were unknown rather than 'household names' created by slick marketing and promotion? Probably not.

So, the name is important. But it can only carry so much weight. In the final analysis, subject, size, medium, period, condition and price still determine, for the most part, the ultimate saleability of a painting. The name simply adds value and desirability to a great painting and gives more than a fighting chance to one that is less than stellar.

Points to Remember:

1. *Famous or well-known artists usually fetch higher prices than their lesser known colleagues.*

2. *Poorer works by known artists can often sell better, because of the name, than good works by minor artists.*

3. *The artist's name is one of the more important factors an auction house considers when establishing an auction estimate.*

4. *Collectors talk about artists, not subjects.*

"for a painting to command a good price... the brush strokes, the style, the perspective, the whole package must ooze quality."

Chapter 6.

An inherent quality has to be there

It is not uncommon for one to see a dreadful painting at auction fetch an astounding price. In such cases, you will usually find that the buyer has not examined the painting properly prior to bidding or is a neophyte in the market and doesn't know what to look for - or just has plain bad taste.

Perhaps the painting was by a prominent artist, or the subject, no matter how poorly executed, was appealing in a sentimental way. Or perhaps two business or neighborhood rivals locked horns to do battle, neither willing to succumb to the other. Whatever the reason, injustice does happen. Bad paintings do get big prices, but not that often and seldom in a sophisticated market.

Never forget that a bad painting, no matter the artist or the current trend, is and always will be a bad painting.

A good painting requires just one essential ingredient. It is not the artist, subject, period, size or even condition. It is the quality.

A Degas canvas of young female dancers preparing to go on stage would hold little market appeal if, upon examination, it looked like he had painted it with his left foot, with his eyes closed, while still trying to recover from a horrendous night on the town that included several carafes of very cheap wine. Well, you get the picture. Even major artists have bad days.

It shouldn't automatically be assumed that, because the painting is by a noted painter, the quality is guaranteed. It isn't. Which is often why, when you look up an artist in a price guide, you will see such disparity between the high and low prices. Of course, there are other factors involved here as well, such as subject, period and size, but quality is what really sets the works apart.

Aunt Agatha's tree may look like a tree, but...

How do we determine quality? That is the million dollar question. To many observers, a tree is a tree. Indeed, Aunt Agatha's tree looks a lot more like a tree than Picasso's, so Aunt Agatha must be a better painter than Picasso. Quality isn't something you can research like a name or drool over like an exhilarating subject - although some art experts do! Quality is an intangible. It is imbedded in originality and creativity. It is something that is either there or it isn't. It's really not something you can teach anyone. Recognizing it comes with experience - and even then, it's not always apparent. It is that certain something, that special magic that the artist has that just makes the painting work.

The dictionary tells us that quality is 'the degree of excellence or relative goodness' in something. In art that excellence is found in the mastery of the brush stroke, the flow of the paint, the control of the brush, the overall balance and composition, the comfortable perspective - that innate artistic knowledge of knowing when to stop. When enough is enough. It is a maturity, a richness, a depth all in one. It is experience. It really cannot be learned, it just is.

An artist either has it or doesn't. The great ones always do. As an observer, you either have the ability to recognize it - feel it would be a better word - or you don't. It is almost a subliminal recognition. It is that extra something that says to you "Yes! this is a good picture!"

How do you know whether your picture has that quality? If you don't, then you can be sure the market will, so don't worry. And never tamper with the painting trying to find or improve the quality. You won't succeed. Leave it alone.

Underneath all the grime, damage and discoloration and behind the perfect subject by a recognized artist, there has to be a quality painting to command a good price. The brush strokes, the style, the perspective, the whole package must ooze quality.

When it does there is a chemistry in the auction room that causes the adrenalin to flow and hearts to pound - and brings smiles to the faces of both the auctioneer and the consignor!

Points to Remember:

1. Bad paintings can get good prices - but usually for all the wrong reasons.

2. For a painting to be 'good,' it must have quality.

3. Quality is what differentiates two seemingly identical pictures, making one worth so much more than the other.

4. Quality is an almost indefinable attribute that an artist and painting have that set them apart from others. It just is!

Notes:

"the who, when and where of a painting will have a definite impact on the eventual 'how much'!"

Chapter 7.

Who, when and where?

The more information you can provide about a painting, the more chance you have of securing a good or better price at auction. Many artists would title, date and sign their works, thus providing us with most of the relevant information we need to know. However, particularly in older works - 19th century and before - it is extremely common for at least one, if not all three, of these ingredients to be missing. This is where a little investigative work on your part could pay handsome dividends.

Buyers, especially first-time purchasers, like to know as much about a painting as possible. It's only human nature. But, more than that, it also adds interest and potential value to a piece, and that's always appealing. It also broadens your market base. Many artists are only popular in certain regions of the country or for certain subjects and even periods.

The date of a painting is especially important for more contemporary works of the 20th century. Here, the difference of a couple of years can mean a difference in selling price of perhaps many thousands of dollars.

Providing as much information about your painting, therefore, makes sound business sense - and it's fun!

If a painting is signed and dated but not titled, then a little research about the artist - perhaps where he was at the time the piece was painted - will give you some definite clues as to where a landscape or coastal view might be. There might also be some tell-tale clues within the painting - such as the steeple of a famous cathedral, or the configuration of a well-known port or harbor - that are instantly recognizable.

If the painting is signed and titled but not dated, then, again, a little research could tell you when the artist was in this particular region, maybe on a sketching trip with other artists. If this is the case, then you can often narrow the date down to a specific year or even time of year.

On the other hand, if the title indicates that the location is a popular one for the artist - many 19th century painters, for instance, would stay in one region all their lives and only paint that region - then setting a date might be more of a challenge. There may, however, be some stylistic clues that will help here.

Perhaps the artist changed the colors in his palette later in his career or adopted a more impressionistic rather than representational technique. Or maybe he worked with a palette knife rather than a brush or vice-versa. In the case of 20th century abstract painters, maybe a particular color, shape or theme became more dominant at a particular stage in the artist's development. If this is the case, then it might be possible to narrow the time frame down to a few specific years.

An intelligent guess is better than no guess at all!

Remember, it is better to have even a general idea of when a painting might have been painted than no idea at all. For instance, if an artist lived between 1835 and 1905, and you are looking at a well-painted, mature canvas, then it would be fairly safe to say that it was probably painted in the late 19th century, perhaps the 1880s or 90s, or around the turn of the century. A less mature work might be dated between 1860 to 1880. It's only guesswork, but it could be substantiated with at least some intelligent evidence - and an intelligent guess is better than no guess at all!

If a painting is unsigned, the task of identification becomes extremely Difficult, verging on the almost impossible. Unless you are an art expert and, more specifically, a specialist in the type of art under examination, the chances of knowing who painted the picture are slim. At best, again, because of several clues - perhaps the piece is titled or dated or has a recognizable locale - you might be able to hazard a very general guess or provide some options. More likely, however, you or the auction house you take it to will only be able to attribute it to a school of art and possibly a country of origin. Once again, something is better than nothing, and anything you can do in the way of research before you take the piece to an auction house will help the auctioneer with his cataloging.

The need for research applies to a portrait as well as to a landscape. Do you know who the sitter is? Identifying the sitter in a portrait can often be more important than identifying the locale in a landscape. This is particularly so with Old Master paintings. The subjects of Old Master and later works were usually either famous people or wealthy local dignitaries and their identification will usually add a great deal of value to the final price of the painting. Because it was quite common for Old Masters to be unsigned, identifying the sitter or sitters might also be an excellent clue to identifying the artist.

How can you research locales, dates or potential artists? Do lots of reading at the local library, and look at as many illustrations of the period as you can find. Old auction catalogues in second- hand bookshops and swap meets are a handy source. One short cut you might consider, when you know the artist but want to date a work or identify a location, is to look in the price guides. Here you'll find other pieces by the artist and likely find similar dates and title descriptions that will provide you with some useful clues.

So, remember, the *Who, When and Where* of a painting will have a definite impact on the eventual *How Much!*

Points to Remember:

1. *The more information you can provide the auctioneer on the subject of your painting, the better price you are likely to achieve.*

2. *Specific locations and names of individuals have more appeal to potential buyers than generalities.*

3. *What you don't know directly about your painting you should try and find out by doing some research.*

4. *Remember, who, when and where are just as important as how much!*

"Who owned the painting can add prestige to a collector's walls and increased value to a dealer's mark-up."

———————

Chapter 8.

Provenance - or from whence does it come?

The history, or provenance, of a painting is another vital piece of information about your picture that could increase its value substantially. If you can trace the previous ownership of your painting to an important or famous person, it will almost certainly add value to the final hammer price.

The more famous the owner, the higher the price. You only have to look at the collector-mania that takes place around celebrity auctions, particularly in the United

States, to see the truth in this. The Jacqueline Onassis auction was perhaps the most glaring example. Here we saw insignificant trinkets fetching the prices of Old Masters and ordinary paintings vying for world records.

Now, it is unlikely that your painting had as illustrious a past as that. Nevertheless, its past, and what you can find out about it will have an impact on the final hammer price. Dealers and collectors, especially the serious ones, like to know as much about the works they buy as possible. The provenance is an important part of that information. Who owned the painting can add prestige to a collector's walls and increased value to a dealer's mark-up.

Knowing a painting's history from the day it was painted is, of course, the best provenance of all. Certainly this is possible in more contemporary works, but it becomes more difficult, verging on almost impossible, for earlier pieces. Some sleuthing through old auction catalogues and price guides could well provide some history but is unlikely to tell it all. Again, something is always better than nothing.

One significant advantage to having a detailed provenance, particularly one that includes a prominent person, be they a well-known collector, celebrity or local dignitary, can be found in the area of authentication. Works that have come from good collections are seldom questioned as to their authenticity. Indeed, the provenance is usually used to enhance the value and certify authenticity. After all, Lord So-And-So would never have a fake in his collection, would he?

Of course, the truth is - yes, he might. Probably unwittingly, but it's definitely possible. Therefore, as a buyer, you should not put too much weight on whose collection a painting came from. Everyone makes mistakes! On the other hand, as a seller, you need to milk it for all it's worth!

A great provenance may also be a great scam

Beware the fake provenance! What you have may not be what you want. Don't be too eager to accept a glowing provenance on your painting when you buy it. If it sounds too good to be true, then it probably is!

And certainly don't be deceived by information scratched onto the stretcher of a painting. Because so many people - auction houses, dealers and collectors alike - put so much emphasis on a painting's provenance, it makes sense for an art criminal to fabricate a provenance to create 'authenticity' for a fake work.

The false provenance may be something as casual as inscribing a recognizable name on the painting's stretcher or suggesting that the piece was exhibited at a major institution, such as the Royal Academy. Or it may be far more complex and devious: tampering with an artist's records in major institutions, creating false exhibition labels, and fabricating relevant correspondence to put the painting in the hands of certain important persons at certain significant times.

Fabricating a false provenance brings to mind the time a colleague purchased a very large and well painted copy of an Old Master 'school of' painting from a Sotheby's Colonnade sale in New York. These are the sales where minor, less valuable works are sold. He had it shipped to his gallery on the west coast and, after several failed attempts to find a private buyer, placed the painting in a local auction, looking to simply get his money back.

To his surprise and delight, the painting sold within estimate, and he was able to get his investment back. Several weeks later, I received a letter from a local collector informing me that a very important 'lost' Old Master had surfaced at a local auction and been purchased by this particular collector.

The collector then proceeded to tell me that the painting had come from a very important local estate, had been in the family for several generations, and was one of only two known versions of this particular subject - a Madonna and child - painted by the artist whose name I have since forgotten. He then told me that the companion work by the artist was to be found in the Rijksmuseum in Amsterdam.

The collector went on to denigrate the expertise and awareness of local dealers and other collectors who all, he pointed out, completely overlooked this hidden masterpiece which, he also informed me, was almost priceless.

Well, he was at least right on the last part. It was almost priceless. Or should that be valueless? I politely informed him of the true history of the painting and put him in touch with my colleague for confirmation. The story and painting quickly disappeared.

It was his bad luck that he happened to contact someone who knew the true story of the painting. But what if he hadn't? Some unsuspecting, naive collector would more than likely have paid a substantial sum to own a rare and important Old Master - that wasn't. And of course, they would have found out the truth several years later, when it was far too late.

Caveat emptor!

Points to Remember:

1. The history of a painting's life (its provenance) is important, especially if it was previously owned by a famous or well known, person.

2. Careful and thorough research can often trace a painting's history back to the original owner.

3. A detailed provenance can be very useful when determining a painting's authenticity.

4. Beware of a fake provenance! Don't be too eager to accept a glowing provenance. If it sounds too good to be true...!

"It is often possible to get as much for an important painting in rural America as it is in London or New York."

———————————

Chapter 9.

Choosing the right auction house

Choosing the right auction house through which to sell your painting, be it within your own community or on a much broader, international scale, can often make the difference between an acceptable price and an exceptional price - or, indeed, any price at all!

As with any field of business, some companies, either because of management, market share, geographic location, or market focus, offer potential clients a better opportunity than their competitors. It is no different in the auction industry. All auction houses are not the same!

It is therefore important to do some research into the best auction house for your particular painting. Most cities have several salerooms from which to chose. Some discreet inquiries on your part will very quickly tell you which of them is the best for you.

If your painting is a minor work, perhaps a good piece by a popular local or even regional artist, then it is important that you find a good saleroom within your community. Look for one that is either known for offering your particular artist's work or holds specific fine art and antique sales rather than general household sessions.

If more than one auction house fits this bill, then the determining factor in which you chose might come down to pay-out time (the period of time following a sale that the auction house takes to pay you for your painting), frequency or timeliness of auctions, the difference in pre-sale estimates, or simply personalities.

Serious paintings deserve a serious audience

For a more serious work, something by an important national artist or a significant international piece, you generally should set your sights much further afield - unless, of course, you happen to live in a major center such as New York or London, where the world's leading auction houses already conduct business.

Serious paintings deserve a serious audience, and those audiences are usually to be found in the larger centers. Company's such as Sotheby's and Christie's have a world-wide clientele to whom to expose your picture, and their very name adds an air of credibility and respectability to your painting.

You should be aware that these salerooms also have higher entry levels, or higher value requirements, than other auction houses. Therefore, if a painting is not of a certain value, even if it is a pleasing, well painted work by a notable artist, then they will not accept it.

The costs of running an auction house are high, and the bigger salerooms have long recognized that they cannot afford to deal in the minor, less valuable works. It takes the same time, catalogue exposure and overhead to sell a minor work as it does a major one - and it is usually easier to sell a major one! - so naturally the salerooms prefer to concentrate on the more expensive works. If this is the case, they will likely refer you to a smaller saleroom in the same city or advise you to sell on your local market.

Being accepted by a major saleroom has significant advantages

This said, the advantages in being accepted by these larger rooms are considerable. Inclusion in their catalogues gives instant respectability and authenticity to your work. The exposure is international. The drawing power of other, more important works in the sale is significant, and the expectation of success is understood. At this level, also, there are many collectors who have a loyalty to one particular saleroom and only consider works offered by that auction house.

Finding the right saleroom within your own region or even country may not present too much of a problem and certainly won't cost you too much when it comes to shipping your work. However, the best auction house for you might well be overseas, and this presents a different situation altogether.

A Scottish Impressionist painting, for example, will almost certainly do better in a specialty sale of Scottish pictures conducted in Glasgow or Edinburgh by Sotheby's or Christie's than it will almost anywhere else. Similarly, a major marine or sporting pictures auction in London would be the right place for important works in these categories, rather than selling on the home market. Often, paintings that sold for relatively little in the smaller, more provincial salerooms around the country have eventually found their way into major catalogue sales in the bigger centers, where they have sold for several times their previous price. To avoid this happening to your painting, you need to research your potential outlet thoroughly.

Don't overlook the cost of shipping overseas

If an overseas saleroom is interested in your painting, it is important to remember the costs and complications of getting it there. This is also true if you have to crate and ship across country rather than simply drive down to your local auction house. What costs are you going to incur to get your work to auction?

Shipping overseas, for example, will not only mean crating and shipping costs, but also insurance, possible import duties at the other end, and local delivery charges when it gets to its country of destination. All these costs, when added together, along with the uncertainty of whether your picture will actually sell or not, could prove prohibitive. After all, the bottom line is what really matters - how much you actually receive for your painting once it has been sold. A lower price on a home market may well prove more profitable for you than a 'glamorous' price on an international market. So you will need to do your math carefully before you jump into shipping overseas.

There's another factor you should consider before you ship either overseas or even across country. What if the painting doesn't sell? How will you get the picture back? The saleroom will usually crate it for you, sometimes without cost, but you will certainly have to pay the shipping and insurance, and from overseas, this could be quite expensive.

So you really have to weigh all the economic pros and cons before you ship a painting away from home. You don't want to become one of the nightmare statistics that pay out more in shipping and handling charges than the painting is worth!

Sell local and minor paintings on the local market

As a general rule of thumb, paintings by local artists should be sold on the local market, as should minor works by national and international artists. Better quality paintings by more renowned national artists should be sold in their home town or region. A quick look in a price guide will often tell you which saleroom sells most of the artist's works. That saleroom likely will be situated within the region where the artist was born, spent most of his life or painted extensively and for which he is now recognized.

Important national or international artists, and especially those with no real regional ties, should be sent to the bigger salerooms in major centers. Again, if the price guides tell you that these pieces get the best prices overseas, then you should consider shipping out of country. You should also consider this option for important specialty works such as marine, wildlife, hunting or topographical works.

95

In all cases, never forget to factor in the cost of getting your work to auction. Attention to this detail could literally turn less into more.

There are advantages to selling big names in small markets

Having said all this, I have to add that there is, of course, an exception to every rule! Today's sophisticated communications systems, such as computers, e-mail, faxes and the like, are quickly becoming an auctioneer's 'weapons' of choice in the highly competitive world of fine art auctioneering. Buyers around the world can be informed of a painting's presence in even the most remote auction house. It is, therefore, often possible to get as much for an important painting in rural America as it is in London or New York.

If the painting is worth it and if the auction house takes advantage of today's technology to reach the world-wide marketplace, then buyers and, more specifically, dealers and serious collectors will either make the trek to the outlying location or bid by phone based on visual data received.

Indeed, sometimes there is even an advantage to selling a more important work in a minor market, although it certainly is much more of a gamble and one that you shouldn't undertake lightly. It is usually dealers that will take the trouble to travel to a less central location. Once there, they seldom like to leave that location empty handed. They need to buy something in order to pay for their trip. As a result, they may well be inclined to spend considerably more than they would have in a bigger, more accessible market to acquire the work they came for.

While the dealer may have to take a lot less future profit than he was hoping for, there will be some consolation in the fact that, for the most part, the painting will be fresh to the major market he's taking it to.

Clearly it is extremely important to make the right saleroom choice. By staying with your local market you not only cut down on costs and expenses, but you might also benefit, if it is an important work, from being the proverbial big fish in a small pond. But there is a risk to this, and the risk may not be worth taking.

By shipping your work nationally or internationally you immediately and substantially increase the size of your potential market. You reach a broader trade and collector market, which may be all you need to ensure your work achieves the best price possible.

But do not be blinded by the expectation of higher prices away from home. Do your homework, pay attention to costs, decide whether you can live with the worst case scenario, and then - and only then - make your decision.

Points to Remember:

1. *Choosing the right auction house through which to sell your painting can make a considerable difference to the price you get.*

2. *Do your research to find out which is the best saleroom for you before you consign.*

3. *As a rule of thumb, sell local works on the local market.*

4. *Consider the costs of shipping versus selling on the local market before you send your painting across country or overseas.*

5. *Don't overlook the costs of return shipment should your painting fail to sell at an outside saleroom.*

6. *Important works should usually be sent to major national or international salerooms.*

7. *There is always an exception to the rule. With today's technology, salerooms can reach collectors around the world at the press of a button. Sometimes, therefore, a good picture, when placed in a small market, can stand out so much it does extremely well - as well as in a major market. It's your call!*

How Do You Make Money Selling Art At Auction?

Don't forget..

1. Paintings by famous or well-known artists usually fetch higher prices than their lesser known colleagues.

2. Collectors talk about the artists in their collection, not the subjects.

3. For a painting to be good it must have 'quality.'

4. Quality is usually what differentiates two seemingly identical pictures making one worth more than the other.

5. The who, where and when of a painting are just as important as the *how much.*

6. The more information you can provide on your painting the better price you are likely to achieve.

7. A painting's provenance is important, especially if it includes a famous person or collection.

8. Beware of fake provenances! If it sounds too good to be true, it probably is.

9. Choosing the right saleroom for your painting can have a major impact on the price you get.

10. You should consider the costs of shipping - both ways! - versus selling on the local market.

*"By illustrating your painting
in the catalogue...you stand to
increase its overall market potential
by as much as 50%..."*

———————

Chapter 10.

Say *yes* to an illustration in an auction catalogue

An auction catalogue is more than just a reference or identification source for viewers at a sale's preview, although that is its primary function. The catalogue also serves as the sale's traveling ambassador. It is the sale away from home. For many collectors and dealers, the catalogue is the only access to the sale. To this potential market - and it can be, and usually is, a vast network of international buyers - perhaps the most important aspect of the catalogue is the illustrations. Illustrated entries attract immediate attention and, therefore, consideration. The very presence of an illustration is also a form of endorsement from the auction house that this is a good painting and certainly one worthy of being illustrated. Color illustrations, as you might expect, carry more impact and serve to heighten the sense of importance and appeal.

No matter how expert you are, it is almost impossible to correctly visualize a painting that is not illustrated. Unless the artist, subject matter, or perhaps low pre-sale estimate is of specific interest to a potential absentee buyer, it is unlikely that he will show any interest in a non-illustrated item. If there is interest, then a phone call to the saleroom will often result in a photo being mailed along with a first-hand condition report. But this is a lot of effort for the saleroom and collector, and unless both parties see a real value or return for this effort, it may ultimately prove to be just too much trouble.

The number of catalogues an auction house produces depends on the size of the saleroom and the importance of the sale. If, for example, the saleroom prints a thousand catalogues prior to an upcoming sale, it is more than likely that as many as 50% of them will reach buyers who will not attend the auction. By illustrating your work in the catalogue, therefore, you stand to increase its overall market potential by the same amount - a substantial share of the market you should not overlook.

You might be able to negotiate
a free illustration

What do illustrations cost? They vary from saleroom to saleroom. Many companies include black and white illustrations for free, but only on works they select. A few will also include free color images, but again the choice belongs to the saleroom. Others charge a small fee for black and white, and the consignor can agree to or decline an illustration. Color has more impact and is much more expensive.

Usually, the saleroom will suggest a color illustration for the more important pieces and perhaps even include it for free as part of the consignment contract if the work is one of the feature lots in the sale. You might also be able to negotiate a special illustration rate if you have multiple works in the auction or, again, a particularly desirable piece that the saleroom is keen to offer.

Many auction houses, usually due to cost controls, do not carry illustrations in their catalogues. Some will only illustrate pre-sale flyers and promotions. But when dealing with those that do, make sure you ask the auctioneer for details. Again, however, do not overlook the costs involved. If an illustration will not effectively and substantially improve the bottom line, don't do it!

Points to Remember:

> **1.** *Say yes to an illustration in the auction catalogue, it's money well spent.*
>
> **2.** *For many collectors, the catalogue is their only way to view a sale. An illustration, therefore, is almost like being at the auction preview for these collectors.*
>
> **3.** *Catalogue descriptions without an illustration can be very deceiving and, therefore, off-putting to many collectors.*
>
> **4.** *Collectors tend to bypass paintings in a catalogue that aren't illustrated.*

"don't be greedy. Take fair market value for your painting - and move on!"

———————————

Chapter 11.

Keep your expectations modest
- and do your homework!

This is probably the most important advice of all when selling a painting through auction - and perhaps the hardest to follow. I've already alluded to this in the chapter on *Estimates and Reserves*, but it is so important it bears repeating. Keep your expectations modest.

Before you approach a saleroom, it is good practice to do some preliminary research of your own - just so there are no surprises. A quick check of available price guides will give you an idea of what you might expect for your painting. Always remember to compare apples with apples, however. And don't make judgment calls such as "Yes, but mine is obviously better than these." It may well be, but let someone else, preferably the auctioneer, make that decision. It is also a good rule to ignore the top one or two prices in the guides. Instead, try and get a sense of the average price for a similar work by the artist, taking into account the size, subject, medium, date, and so on.

If the price isn't right for you
- don't consign

Once you have completed your research, it is time to listen to the auctioneer. Be guided by his expertise and the values he suggests. He will, in all likelihood, base his initial valuation on the same averages you have already recognized. Then he will add or subtract from these values, depending on the various other criteria we have previously discussed in this book: artist, subject, size, condition, provenance, etc. If his final conclusion is a satisfactory price to you, then any greater price your work might achieve will be a pleasant bonus. If the auctioneer's price is less than you expected and are prepared to accept, then don't consign it. The time or the circumstances are obviously not right for you.

Don't try and create the price you want by insisting on a high reserve. It will almost surely backfire. A high reserve means a high estimate and that will be enough to discourage buyers. The result - the dreaded *BI*!.

To add insult to injury, you may well incur additional costs associated with your painting's failed attempt to find a buyer. Costs, such as illustration fees, shipping, insurance, and return freight charges, can all add up to a very expensive and frustrating experience - all because you wanted more than the market felt was your fair share!

The net result is that you will be out of pocket either financially or through loss of time and effort - and all you will have to show for it is the reappearance of your painting back on your walls, probably for some time to come.

So, don't be greedy. Take fair market value for your painting - and move on!

Points to Remember:

1. *Keep your expectations modest.*

2. *Do your homework before you consign your painting, but be sensible. Do not assume your painting is on a par with the most expensive works in an auction price guide. It may be, but don't make the assumption.*

3. *Listen to the auctioneer, he knows his market.*

4. *If you don't like the price quoted by the auctioneer, don't consign.*

5. *Don't be greedy! Take fair market value for your painting - and move on!*

"the chances of selling your painting
for more than $500 increase
substantially to almost three in five"

Chapter 12.

What will you get for your painting?

The answer to this question will, of course, not be known until the auctioneer brings the gavel down at the end of bidding. However, statistics tell us that a large percentage of paintings sold at auction have trouble reaching their pre-sale estimates. Many might appear to do so when the auction house adds its 10% or 15% buyer's premium to the hammer price. This premium, however, is strictly for the auction house. The hammer price is the figure you will be paid out on - less, of course, the auctioneer's commission and any other incurred costs, such as illustrations, insurance and the like.

In most cases, the hammer price is somewhere between the low estimate and the reserve, which, as we have mentioned in an earlier chapter, is normally set at about 80% of the low estimate. A painting, therefore, that is estimated at $1000-1500 will usually have a reserve of around $800 and will more than likely sell between $800 and $1000.

Several paintings, of course, will sell within estimate, though often at the lower end, while a privileged few - usually attractive or important works with reasonable estimates - will have the honor and distinction of finding a buyer above estimate - sometimes well above. Your preliminary research, together with discussions with the auctioneer, will give you a fairly accurate indication of what you might expect for your painting.

Remember: most paintings sell for less than $2000!

Most people, understandably, have high expectations for the paintings they send to auction. They are optimistic - and definitely hopeful - that their works are really different from all the rest and will beat the odds - odds, like a trip to a casino, that are seemingly heavily stacked against them. For the harsh reality is that most paintings in North America will sell for less than $2000 (1000 pounds in the U.K.), and the vast majority of these will not even reach the $1000 level.

According to statistics released in Canada by the *Canadian Art Sales Index**, 78.9% of paintings sold during the 1998-99 auction season in Canada sold for $2000 or less! That's almost four out of every five paintings sold.

Close to half of the season's sales - 47.8% - sold for $1000 or less.

Perhaps a more telling statistic can be found in the number of paintings that sold for $500 or less - 44.9%, more than two out of five. When you take into consideration the fact that the *Canadian Art Sales Index* does not record any works that sold for less than $50, you can see that, in all likelihood, these figures are far more conservative than aggressive.

What does all this mean to you? It means that your chances of selling your painting for more than $2000 are one in five, or 20%! But your chances of selling for more than $500 increase substantially to almost three in five, or over 55%. If you are expecting more than $2000, then you better be sure you have all the right ingredients to give your painting the necessary market edge.

*Although these figures relate specifically to the Canadian art market, reports from the U.S. and U.K. show similar statistics, with close to 80% of the market conducted at the low end.

Points to Remember:

1. *Most paintings that sell do so somewhere between the reserve and low estimate.*

2. *Close to 80% of all paintings sell for less than $2000 (1000 pounds in the U.K.).*

3. *Almost 50% of all paintings sell for less than $1000 (500 pounds).*

4. *Keep your expectations reasonable. Let the market decide.*

"In just a few short years, online auctions have accumulated annual sales surpassing the world-wide sales for both Sotheby's and Christie's"

Chapter 13.

Electronic auctions - or selling art on the internet

Quietly and decisively, an exciting new way to buy and sell at auction has crept into our homes via the computer. So rapid has been the growth of online auctions and so huge the reported sales (researchers predict that online auction sales will reach $19 billion by 2003!) that all of the world's leading live salerooms are paying serious attention to its progress and development.

With this new medium still in its formative stages, it is uncertain whether it will be considered suitable for all levels of the antiques and art market. We already know that collectibles, multiples and low-end antiques and art are finding a vast international marketplace on the net. And even works in the low to mid thousands of dollars are being scooped up by an ever expanding buyer market. But the jury is still out on how well higher end goods, especially fine paintings and antiques, will do. Some things really do need to be seen and examined in person.

Attending an auction from the comfort of your home is appealing and entertaining

The idea of buying and selling from the comfort of your home, with little or no expense involved, is attractive and entertaining to seasoned and new collectors alike. Millions of objects are being offered each day on the internet simultaneously by several electronic auction companies who are generating billions of dollars a year in sales. Latest figures show online auction sales accounting for about 20% of all internet commerce.

Companies such as eBay, uBid, eHammer, Artnet, Finelot and numerous others are leading this new facet of the auction industry, and new ones are entering the market at an amazing pace. But the giants are not far behind. Both Sotheby's and Christie's, who together generate over $4 billion in annual sales through their live auctions, are now making their presence felt in this new and extremely lucrative market, as are Phillips, Bonhams, Butterfields and other leading U.S. and European salerooms.

Sotheby's has already launched its up-scale site, sothebys.com, and has joined forces with another online business giant - amazon.com - to form a separate site - sothebys.amazon.com - dealing mostly in lower- end collectibles and memorabilia.

For years, Sotheby's and Christie's stayed away from the low end of the antiques and fine art market because the profit, or commission, margins were too slim. They found that, in terms of time, labor and exposure, it cost as much to sell a $100,000 painting as it did a $1000 item. With the extremely low operating costs associated with the internet, the lower end of the art market - which accounts for about 80% of market activity - suddenly looks more attractive to these saleroom giants.

Because of the ease with which the general public can view and buy through online auctions, the size of the buying market is enormous. It is also, for the most part, unsophisticated. The result is a marked lack of market and product knowledge playing havoc with real market values. Many items are selling for several times their real worth, as buyers treat the auction process more like a game than a serious purchasing medium.

Lack of policing the main drawback to online trading

While the participation in online auctions of the major leading live auction houses adds a great deal of credibility and control to the process, there is still a long way to go before buying and selling through the electronic medium will be considered a safe and desirable alternative to live auctions. One of the main problems facing this industry at the present time is the lack of policing by the e-salerooms on the goods they sell, the consignors they do business with, and the satisfactory fulfillment of each transaction.

As with any fledgling industry, especially one that has grown and continues to grow so fast, there is no shortage of unscrupulous individuals eager to take advantage of its teething pains and difficulties. Horror stories abound, particularly in the areas of authentication, description and perceived value, as well as in the delivery - or in many cases the non-delivery - of goods purchased.

A panel of fine art experts was gathered together by the *Wall Street Journal* in 1999 to examine several of the online auction sites. Their findings were not encouraging. As many as half the items in certain categories were misrepresented, inaccurately priced, or so poorly described as to make informed bidding practically impossible. That applied as much to the high-end items as it did to the lower priced collectibles. The experts also noticed several high-priced bids on items they considered to be nothing more than junk.

Inaccurate pricing is not always a failing. One consignor listed a Pueblo clay pot from the 1920s for $24.95 on eBay. The pot was discovered to have been made by a famous period artist and bidding closed at $77,000.

Screening of goods difficult when millions of items are being offered

The problem lies in the fact that it is very difficult for online auctions to effectively screen the goods they offer for accuracy or authenticity. And, while most say they want to get rid of the fraud, none, apart from the major live salerooms, yet has any plans to begin vetting merchandise. When you consider that, at any one time the leading online auction house eBay has almost 2 million items up for bid, and 10 million customers, it becomes clear why these electronic salerooms cannot take responsibility for all they offer.

To their credit, however, some online auctions, eBay being one of them, are making a concerted effort to improve the quality of service and authenticity of items offered by instituting more rigid registration procedures. By asking sellers for a credit card number or other accepted form of identification the company is hoping to ensure that all bidders are of legal age and take a responsible and serious approach to selling items on the net.

In just a few short years, online auctions have accumulated annual sales surpassing the world-wide sales for both Sotheby's and Christie's, both of which were founded in the 18th century. With such unprecedented growth, it is inevitable that this electronic medium will ultimately completely change the way we conduct business at auction.

How does all this information on online auctions affect you? Well, if you decide to sell your painting over the internet, you might want to consider one of the bigger names first - especially if your work has some real value to it. If, on the other hand, your painting is borderline, with perhaps an uncertain or unknown provenance and maybe a little weak in the quality or name department, then selling it on the net may be just the way to go. Commissions are definitely a lot lower than in conventional salerooms and the exposure is far greater. eBay charges an insertion fee of around $2, and a modest selling fee based on the final price: 5% on the first $25, 2.5% on the next $975, and 1.25% on the remaining balance - for example, an item selling for $1500 costs the seller just $31.88. It's also easy to do.

Check out as many auction websites as you can to find out what they have to offer. Many, while advertising art and antique auctions, leave a lot to be desired when it comes to quality and numbers of items offered. Established online salerooms already have a strong customer clientele so try and pick a site, or sites, that offer works of a similar quality and price range to yours to take full advantage of this client base.

After you have registered with an online site you need to list the painting, or paintings, you wish to sell. Most sellers include an illustration of the item, although it is possible to sell online without one. As the seller you set your own reserve, but you will encourage more bidding if you do not have one. Auctions vary in length but most last about seven days, so make sure you know all the rules and regulations before you sign up.

If your painting sells online you will then discover the purchaser's identity and the two of you will make arrangements for shipping and payment.

Most online auctions employ what we know as the 'silent' auction method. Bidders can go back time and again as the price rises to increase their bids for the duration of the sale. Most of the action, however, as you might expect, takes place just before the sale is scheduled to end. Serious bidders then watch eagerly to see if their bid is going to be successful - while you watch the action on your painting from the comfort of your own home.

The latest twist to online auctions are virtual auctions. Here, you actually participate in the sale as it happens. It is conducted like a live auction, lot by lot, only the bidding is done over the internet. Many live auctions are also attracting real time internet bidders who work through an agent who is actually attending the sale, taking instructions through a laptop or other computer.

If you decide to try an online auction and are not successful, then you can always withdraw the work and proceed through normal channels to sell it at a live sale with little or no risk of it having been overexposed.

Points to Remember:

1. Online auctions are still too new for us to gauge how successful they will be in selling higher-end art works.

2. Because of the rapid growth and huge sales of this new auction phenomenon, there are unscrupulous business people taking advantage of unsuspecting buyers and sellers. Extreme caution is advised.

3. If you decide to sell a quality work over the internet, consider approaching the bigger names in the industry first, such as Sotheby's or Christie's.

4. Online auctions offer a huge international market with little cost.

5. If you are not successful selling online, you can always revert to the more conventional live auction process without fear of overexposure for your work.

"if you have done your research..
the price you receive from the dealer
will be what you might expect from
the auction - or better."

———————————————

Chapter 14.

Selling to and through the trade

What are the alternatives to selling your art through auction? You could sell privately to friends or to the general public through advertisements in trade publications or local classifieds. You could donate your painting to a charitable institution and receive a tax credit. This might be the way to go if you have a difficult painting to sell or one that has strong retail value but little or no secondary market interest.

Your best alternative, however, is to sell your painting to, or through, the fine art trade.

There are many advantages to selling your painting to and through an art dealer. Perhaps the most important is the fact that you will receive immediate payment when you sell your work directly to the dealer, whereas at auction, you could wait up to two months to be paid out. If you consign your painting to a gallery, rather than selling it outright, you will not be paid until the piece sells and that could be weeks or even months - perhaps longer. If you choose the consignment route, therefore, while it is usual for you to receive more for your item than by selling outright (because the dealer doesn't have to invest any of his own money into it), you should not be in any hurry to get paid.

Selling to the trade can offer security

Another advantage in selling to the trade is the guaranteed sale. There is no uncertainty as there is with the auction. It is a *fait accompli*! And, if you have done your research thoroughly, you will know that the price you receive from the dealer will be what you might expect from the auction - or better. The only unknown is whether you might have received more at auction. But that is offset by the assurance that you didn't get less at auction or, indeed, fail to sell altogether.

There is also the matter of costs of sale. By taking your painting to an art dealer, your costs of sale are zero. You spend nothing on the painting before you take it in. You don't incur any packing or shipping costs (even when you sell it to an out-of-town gallery, the dealer will usually pay all the related shipping costs), and there are no illustration and commission fees to deduct. The price for which you sell your painting is the price you receive.

Selling through the art trade is also more private, and you have more control over the outcome. What is more, if you choose the gallery consignment route and the painting does not sell after a specified period of time, its reputation will not have been damaged through over-exposure the way it would have been had it failed to sell at auction. It also leaves it wide open for you to take it to auction if the trade cannot produce the result you want. Failing at auction and then trying to find a dealer to take the work is a far more difficult task to perform.

A word of caution. As with salerooms, all dealers are not alike! Do your due diligence before you approach a gallery. You want to be sure you are dealing with an honest and reputable dealer with the specialized market knowledge you need. It is also important, from a human standpoint, to enjoy a feeling of friendship and trust with the dealer.

Points to Remember:

1. *Other options to consider, if you chose not to sell your painting through auction, include art dealers, donation and private sales.*

2. *Art dealers can offer you immediate payment and a guaranteed sale.*

3. *There are no 'hidden' costs when selling outright to an art dealer.*

4. *Selling to and through an art dealer can offer more privacy and confidentiality.*

5. *Do your due diligence - not all dealers, nor all auction houses, are the same!*

"no matter how you decide to sell your painting...you can improve your chances of a higher overall net return when you know 'How to Make Money Selling Art at Auction'"

In conclusion...

One can never second-guess the art market. It alone dictates what it will pay for a particular painting on any given day, in any given location. It may well be that your painting deserves to be one of the low-end statistics. If this is so, then there is no doubt that you can greatly improve its odds of achieving the best price possible by following many of the tips covered in this book.

If your painting is important, of quality, painted by a notable artist, or especially appealing because of its subject matter, then it may well be destined to be one of the 10% or 20% of works that perform above expectations. Such works will also benefit greatly from the advice in this book.

Indeed, no matter how you decide to sell your painting - at auction, online, privately, through a dealer - you can improve your chances of a higher overall net return when you know *How to Make Money Selling Art at Auction.*

Good luck - and may the gavel always fall favorably for you!

artstats.com

Appendices

Notes:

Auction terminology:

Auction - a public sale in which the price is increased by bids until the highest bidder becomes the purchaser.

Auction catalogue - the document produced by an auction house that itemizes all objects in the sale. The catalogue often includes pre-sale estimates and illustrations of many of the works on offer.

Auctioneer - the person who conducts the auction sale and takes the bids.

Auction house - the company that organizes and conducts the auction.

Auction preview - the period of time set aside by an auction house for potential bidders to examine the works in a sale prior to their being offered at auction. The preview can be as short as an hour or as long as a week. In the case of a celebrity or extremely important auction, the preview might be longer.

Buyer's premium - a commission charged by the auction house on top of the hammer price. Usually 10% or 15%.

Buy in (BI) - a painting that does not sell when sent to auction because it does not receive a bid equal to or greater than its reserve or, if there is no reserve, fails to attract any bids at all, is considered to have been 'bought in' by the auction house and remains the property of the owner. The figure at which an auctioneer 'buys in' a painting - the bought in price - is the price upon which an auction house can charge a buy in fee, usually 5%.

Caveat emptor - buyer beware.

Consignment commission - the fee charged to the consignor by the auction house for selling a lot. The percentage charged varies among auction houses and according to the value of goods sold. The consignment commission is deducted from the hammer price before a consignor is paid.

Estimates - a price range assigned to a painting prior to the auction and within which the auction house believes the painting will sell.

Gavel - a mallet or other wooden object used by the auctioneer to knock on the podium top signaling the completion of bidding on a particular lot or object.

Hammer price - the price for which a painting is knocked down prior to the buyer's premium being added.

Knock down - the act of closing the bidding on a lot by knocking the gavel on the podium top.

Lot - item for sale. Each item in an auction is assigned a lot number, and lots are sold in numeric order.

Online auctions - auctions conducted on the internet. These are usually silent auctions, although virtual auctions are becoming more common.

On the auction block - put up for auction. The block refers to the surface - usually a table or podium - upon which the auctioneer knocks his gavel.

Primary market - the first market for a painting. Applies mostly to contemporary paintings by living artists which can be found in an art gallery.

Provenance - the history of a painting. Who has owned it and where it has been prior to its present consignor.

Real time bidding - bidding online for items being sold in real time at a live auction sale.

Reserve - that price, agreed upon by the auctioneer and the consignor, below which a painting cannot be sold. Usually set at 80% of the low estimate.

Saleroom - auction house.

Secondary market - the market where paintings are re-sold or traded for the second time or more. This market usually refers to the auction industry or art dealers who specialize in re-sale items.

Silent auctions - auctions that invite 'silent' or written bids over an extended period of time - perhaps a few hours, days, or even weeks. Bidders list the price they want to pay for an object so that other potential bidders can see the bid and, if interested, improve upon the bid. A bidder can raise the bid as often as he likes until the auction is closed off by the auctioneer. Most internet auctions are silent auctions.

The trade - art dealers who deal in secondary market paintings.

Virtual auctions - auctions that are conducted in a 'live' format but which cater to buyers bidding over the internet.

Fine Art Auction Houses:

There are few regions in the United States, Canada and the United Kingdom where there isn't an auction house within a readily accessible distance. Most mid to large towns and cities have one or more local salerooms, and most larger centers have a selection of specialty fine art auction houses. Among the more prominent of these fine art salerooms are:

United States:

Frank H. Boos Gallery
420 Enterprise Court
Bloomfield, Michigan 48013
(313)332-1500
www.boosgalery.com

Butterfield & Butterfield
220 San Bruno Avenue
San Francisco, California
94103 (415)861-7500
www.butterfields.com

Christie, Manson & Woods International, Inc.
20 Rockefeller Plaza
New York, New York 10020
(212)636-2000
www.christies.com

Christie's East
219 East 67th Street
New York, New York 10021
(212)606-0400
www.christies.com

William Doyle Galleries
175 East 87th Street
New York, New York 10128
(212)427-2730
www.doylegalleries.com

Du Mouchelle Art Galleries
409 E. Jefferson
Detroit, Michigan 48226
(313)963-6255
www.dumouchelles.com

Freeman/Fine Arts Company
1808 - 10 Chestnut Street
Philadelphia, Pennsylvania
19103 (215)563-9275

Guernsey's
108 East 73rd Street
New York, New York 10021
(212)794-2280
www.guernseys.com

Phillips Son & Neale, Inc.
406 East 79th Street
New York, New York 10021
(212)570-4830
www.phillips-auction.com

Skinner Inc.
357 Main Street
Bolton, Massachusetts 01740
(978)779-6241
www.skinnerinc.com

C.G. Sloan & Company, Inc.
4920 Wyaconda Road
North Bethesda, Maryland
20852 (301)468-4911
www.sloansauction.com

Sotheby's, Inc.
1334 York Avenue
New York, New York 10021
(212)606-7000
www.sothebys.com

Sotheby's Arcade Auctions
1334 York Avenue
New York, New York 10021

(212)606-7516
www.sothebys.com

Swann Galleries
104 East 25th Street
New York, New York 10010
(212)254-4710
www.swanngalleries.com

Weschler's
909 East Street N.W.
Washington, D.C. 20004
(202)628-1281
www.weschlers.com

Wolf's Auction Gallery
1239 West 6th Street
Cleveland, Ohio 44113
(216)575-9653
www.ewolf.com

Canada:

Christie's Canada
170 Bloor Street W.
Toronto, Ontario M5S 1T9
(416)960-2063
www.christies.com

Arthur Clausen & Sons
11802 - 145th Street
Edmonton, Alberta T5L 2H3
1(877)451-4549
www.clausenauction.com

Empire Auctions
5500 Par Street
Montreal, Quebec H4P 2M1
(514)737-6586
www.empireauctions.com

Galvins Auction
5678 Burleigh Crescent S.E.
Calgary, Alberta T2H 1Z8
(403)253-9401
www.galvinauction.com

Gardner Galleries
186 York Street
London, Ontario N6A 1B5

(519)439-3333
www.gardnergalleries.com

Heffel Fine Art Auction House
2247 Granville Street
Vancouver, B.C. V6H 3G1
(604)732-6505
www.heffel.com

Hodgins Art Auctions
5240 - 1A Street S.E.
Calgary, Alberta T2H 1J1
(403)252-4362
www.hodginsauction.com

Iegor de Saint Hippolyte
2835 Bates Street
Montreal, Quebec H3S 1B3
(514)344-4081
www.iegor.net

Joyner Fine Art Inc.
222 Gerrard Street East
Toronto, Ontario M5A 2E8
(416)323-0909

Levis Art Auctions
#128, 1711 - 10 Avenue S.W.
Calgary, Alberta T3C 0K1
(403)541-9099
www.levisauctions.com

Lunds Auctioneers
926 Fort Street,
Victoria, B.C. V8V 3K2
1(800)363-5863
www.lunds.com

Maynards Auction
415 West 2nd Avenue
Vancouver, B.C. V5Y 1E3
(604)876-6787
www.maynards.com

Phillips Ward-Price Ltd.
16 Ozark Crescent
Toronto, Ontario M4K 1T5
(416)462-9004
www.phillips-auctions.com

Pinney's
2435 Duncan
Montreal, Quebec H4P 2A2
(514)345-0571
www.auctions-on-line.com/pin-neys/auct/index.html

Ritchie's
288 King Street East
Toronto, Ontario M5A 1K4
(416)364-1864
www.ritchies.com

Sotheby's Canada, Inc.
9 Hazelton Avenue
Toronto, Ontario M5R 2E1
(416)926-1774
www.sothebys.com

Waddington's
111 Bathurst Street East
Toronto, Ontario M5V 2R1
(416)504-9100
www.waddingtonsauctions.com

Walker's
18 - 81 Auriga Drive
Nepean, Ontario K2E 7Y5
(613)224-5814
www.walkersauctions.com

United Kingdom:

Bonham's
Montpelier Street
London, SW7 1HH
(171)393 3916
www.bonhams.com

Christie's International
8 King Street, St. James's
London, SW1Y 6QT
(020)7839 9060
www.christies.com

Phillips
101 New Bond Street
London, W1Y 0AS
(171)629-6602
www.phillips-auctions.com

Sotheby's International
34-35 New Bond Street
London W1A 2AA
(020)7293 5000
www.sothebys.com

International Auctioneers Association

Bukowskis
Arsenalsgatan 4 Box 1754 111
87 Stockholm, Sweden
46 861 40 800
www.bukowskis.se

Dorotheum
Palais Dorotheum
Dorotheergasse 17 1010
Vienna, Austria
43 (1) 51560-200
www.dorotheum.com

Etude Tajan
37, rue des Mathurins 75008
Paris, France
33 (1) 53 30 30 00
www.tajan.com

Finarte
Piazzetta Maurilio Bossi, 4
20121 Milan, Italy
39 (02) 877041
www.finarte.it

Galerie Koller
Hardturmstrasse 102 8031
Zurich, Switzerland
41 (1) 445 63 75
www.galeriekoller.ch

Lempertz
Neumarkt 3 50667
Cologne, Germany
49 (221) 92 57 29-0
www.lempertz.com

Butterfields
(See United States listing)

Swann Galleries
(See United States listing)

Not sure whether your painting is suitable auction material, or which saleroom you should take it to?

Why not let us help you?

Anthony Westbridge, President of Westbridge Publications Ltd. is an art auction consultant and author of *How to Make Money Selling Art at Auction*. Let him help you find the right market for your painting. By providing photographs and specific information on your painting, he and his staff will research the best auction or market solution for you.

For complete details on our art auction consultancy service please contact:

Anthony Westbridge
Westbridge Publications Ltd.
1737 Fir Street, Vancouver, B.C. V6J 5J9
Tel: (604)736-1014 Fax: (604)734-4944
e-Mail: info@ westbridge-fineart.com
Web site: www.westbridge-fineart.com